The Power of the Voice
A Guidebook to Find, Regain, and Use Your Unique Sound

Published by:
James Vincent III
Printed in USA

ISBN: 978-0-9986413-7-9

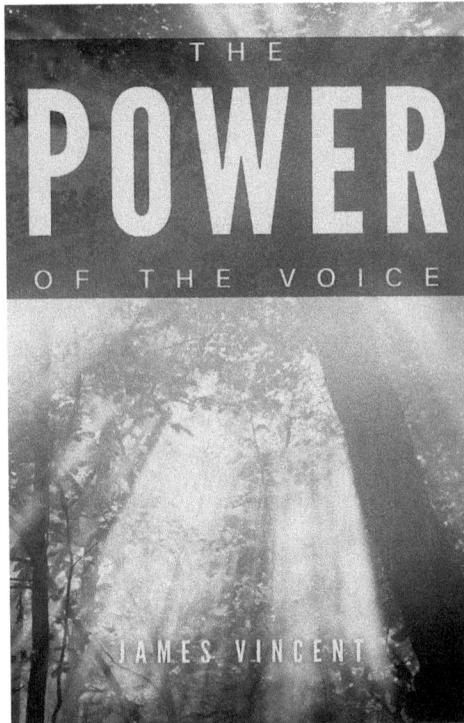

The Power of the Voice Guidebook

This guidebook is designed to inspire you in every way. This great resource will call you to a higher level and cause you to soar beyond the boundaries of the world that you've known. It's time to take flight! Enjoy the journey of exploring the real you as you intentionally begin to discover and understand the power of your voice.

"Using what I've learned on my own journey, I want to help you release the fears and other issues ailing you inwardly. This workbook will be used as a tool, reference guide and handbook to keep you on the path of establishing or regaining your authentic voice and identity. As you consider your notes and answers to each question, be as thorough, honest, and vulnerable as you can be. Be ready to confront root issues and embark on a journey to freedom!"
~ James Vincent, Author, *The Power of the Voice*

Table of Contents

Chapter 1.........................Silence

Chapter 2.........................Voice Raiders: The Silence Begins

Chapter 3.........................Voice Raiders: The Conformity Clause

Chapter 4.........................Grief and Trauma

Chapter 5.........................Finding Your Voice: Purpose Awakens

Chapter 6.........................Finding Your Voice: The Mask Comes Off

Chapter 7.........................Finding Your Voice: The Big Squeeze

Chapter 8.........................Regaining Your Voice: Break Free

Chapter 9.........................The Power of the Voice

The Story Of A New Beginning

Areas Of Your Life Exercise

Goals and Aspirations

Affirmations

The Conclusion

Chapter 1.
Silence

1. As a professional musician and singer, I sang and touched many hearts for years, but still had a very suppressed personality. There was a silence on the inside that controlled my emotions and responses to life. Have you ever felt suppressed by inner silence even when you appeared to be vocal in other areas of your life? How and when?

_____

_____

_____

_____

_____

_____

_____

_____

2. What is silence? Is silence simply *the absence of sound*? Is silence simply *not speaking up when you should*? Define silence in your own words. Use your personal experience to shape your definition.

_____

_____

_____

_____

_____

_____

_____

<u>POWER POINT</u>

*"One of the definitions of silence in the Merriam-Webster Dictionary is **oblivion; obscurity**. **Oblivion** connotates something that is forgotten, not used, or even thought about; it's also the state of being altogether dazed or unaware of the world around you. **Obscurity**, in simplest terms, is more or less being in an unknown or unclear state. So in effect, when I decided to keep my voice oppressed, I was boring a hole deeper and deeper into oblivion and obscurity."*

- James Vincent

The Power of the Voice

3. If one is not living out the true purpose for which he was born, he is living in a state of silence. To be oblivious is to be in a dazed-like state. In what ways do you believe that you are floating in a limbo-false reality, allowing your voice to come under the suppression and oppression of silence?

_____

_____

_____

_____

_____

_____

_____

_____

_____

_____

_____

_____

POWER POINT

"The issue of the voice goes so much deeper than a sound created by air and vibrations of the larynx; it is more than what people hear when you open your mouth to speak, sing, or shout. It is inseparably linked to your identity; the purpose for which you were born."

- James Vincent

4. Your voice is linked to your identity, the purpose for which you were born. Like the character in the book, Herman, have you ever become content with your voice being silenced? Did it ever leave you feeling insecure or unsure of your identity? How? Please explain.

_____

_____

_____

_____

_____

_____

_____

_____

_____

_____

_____

_____

NOTES:

_____

_____

_____

_____

_____

_____

_____

_____

_____

_____

_____

The Power of the Voice

_____

_____

_____

_____

_____

_____

_____

_____

_____

_____

_____

_____

_____

_____

The Power of the Voice

Chapter 2.
Voice Raiders: The Silence Begins

1. How does giving away control of your voice affect you, personally? Do you allow the fear of others to cause you to conform, or are you prone to respond negatively to those you feel are attacking your identity? Explain.

_____

_____

_____

_____

_____

POWER POINT

"An interesting study is how our personalities are shaped by our environment, not only as children, but even into adulthood. We learn, respond, relate many times because of what is afforded to us in our atmosphere. "

- James Vincent

2. Many of us experience "personality demons" as a result of our vocal prison. What are some of the "demons" that you've experienced/are experiencing? List them below.

The Power of the Voice

11

_____

_____

_____

_____

_____

3. When it is time to speak up for yourself, do you struggle? Why? What are some of the emotions you feel? Do you overcome these emotions with a positive or negative response?

_____

_____

_____

_____

_____

4. As we read about the History of Kenya, we learned that there was a cultural assimilation that caused their true identity to be lost in the silence. Can you describe ways that your identity has been lost through a form of assimilation?

_____

_____

_____

_____

_____

5. When referring to the teenage victim of rape towards the end of the chapter, we learn that she was able to move past the oppression of her traumatic history because of her personality that doesn't allow her to remain imprisoned. List some of the things that you learn from this type of individual.

.

_____

_____

_____

_____

_____

NOTES:

_____

_____

_____

_____

_____

_____

_____

_____

_____

_____

_____

_____

_____

_____

_____

_____

_____

_____

_____

_____

_____

_____

Chapter 3.
Voice Raiders: The Conformity Clause

1. Identify the areas of your life that are *wrongly* based on someone else's ideas, causing you to conform and live small. Then identify the areas that are fully based on your personal creativity, vision and intelligence.

_____

_____

_____

_____

_____

2. Take an inventory of your life and ask yourself these questions. Am I stuck? Where am I? How did I get here? What have I learned along the way? What have I gained or lost along the way during this journey?

_____

_____

_____

_____

_____

3. How can I use the things above to help myself get out of a rut?

_____

_____

_____

_____

_____

_____

POWER POINT

"I had to get above every opposing attitude or thing that would attempt to dictate any viability or non-viability of my dreams. I purposed to set myself on the offensive against the silencers that would otherwise cause a regression into the world I had already felt I was failing in."

- James Vincent

4. Are you living below your potential because you're judging yourself according to the measurement of the world's value system? Why or why not?

_____

_____

_____

_____

_____

_____

_____

_____

5. The **Conformity Clause** guarantees you some level of success in freedom, as long as you come under a level of restriction and duplication. Has this affected you? How?

_____

_____

_____

_____

_____

_____

_____

_____

POWER POINT

*"Once I realized that this world was so much bigger than another man's standard, I felt that much more liberty to **just be**."*

- James Vincent

6. The first thing I had to do to break free from the _Conformity Clause_ was to stop fearing the repercussions of taking that leap [of breaking free]. List the fears and concerns you are ready to confront and leap over.

_____

_____

_____

_____

_____

_____

_____

_____

_____

POWER POINT

"So many of us are simply ready to drop all that we are just because someone shows disapproval of our voice. It may be hard to believe, but we all have something to offer. Your sound is important."

- James Vincent

NOTES:

_____

_____

_____

_____

_____

_____

_____

_____

_____

_____

_____

_____

_____

_____

_____

_____

The Power of the Voice

_____

_____

_____

_____

_____

_____

_____

_____

_____

The Power of the Voice

Chapter 4.
Voice Raiders: Grief and Trauma

1. When we deny ourselves the time to heal from trauma, we remain stuck in our grief. Do you feel like you have given yourself the time to heal from past traumatic experiences? If so, how? If not, why?

_____

_____

_____

_____

_____

_____

_____

_____

<u>*POWER POINT*</u>

"Our voice was created to be heard. even if it's not functioning the way it should, it doesn't negate the fact that it was meant to create some sound. and the same way, we were created with the ability to heal. We were created with some intrinsic power to sustain injury, find what we need to overcome that injury, and come through, sometimes more resilient than before."

- James Vincent

2. Many times, we are not willing to face the process of doing the grief work. Unknowingly, this is how we decide to remain in the place of deep woundedness and suffer the consequences of resisting the healing process. What are some of the consequences that we may suffer when we are unwilling to do the grief work that is necessary to heal?

_____

_____

_____

_____

_____

_____

_____

_____

_____

3. The late Maya Angelou suffered a very traumatic experience and she was younger. As a result, she entered what is called selective mutism - a comfortable place of escape from fear that causes you to remain silent, although you have the full ability to speak. Examine your life, have you entered into selective mutism when it comes to certain areas of your life? If so, explain.

_____

_____

_____

_____

_____

_____

_____

_____

_____

4. Here are a few discussion questions to bring clarity and understanding when you feel that your voice is unnaturally being misdirected or shut down. Why does this upset me? Why do I come up in situations like the one I'm in? Why does this make me fearful? Why do I find it hard to forgive or move past a certain situation?

_____

_____

_____

_____

_____

_____

POWER POINT

"Choose not to let yourself live in a state where some past experience has control over areas of your life that should be showing more vibrancy. Remember that healing is natural. Not healing is unnatural."

- James Vincent

NOTES:

_____

_____

_____

_____

_____

_____

_____

_____

_____

_____

_____

_____

_____

_____

_____

_____

_____

_____

The Power of the Voice

_____

_____

_____

_____

_____

_____

_____

Chapter 5.
Finding Your Voice: Purpose Awakens

1. If you are going to find your purpose, you've got to grasp hold of the mindset of living for something greater than yourself. What are you living for that is greater than yourself? What causes you to focus more outwardly than inwardly? Explain why.

_____

_____

_____

_____

_____

_____

_____

_____

_____

_____

POWER POINT

"Somehow, purpose will be introduced to you,...It will basically walk up and shake your hand, ask you a question and whisper in your ear. It will wake you up to a part of you that seemed to be asleep, or awaken a desire to obtain all the tools you need to stand in it."

- James Vincent

2. When new opportunities arise for purpose and identity to be revealed, you should not shy away from them. The more you welcome them, the more you perceive your purpose when these opportunities present themselves. Describe your normal reaction to new opportunities. Why? What are you willing to change?

_____

_____

_____

_____

_____

_____

_____

_____

POWER POINT

"If you are a prisoner in this, remember that you are choosing to be a prisoner. You do have a choice. As painful as it may become, PUSH HARD against despair, PUSH HARD against whatever is oppressing and imprisoning you, PUSH HARD to reach the light of purpose."

- James Vincent

3. Once we allow our purpose to help define our identity, and our identity to define our purpose, many significant and positive things can begin to take place as a result. Describe some of those things below. You can also include personal aspirations. These are some of the things you should intentionally keep before you as you advance in life.

_____

_____

_____

_____

_____

_____

_____

_____

_____

_____

POWER POINT

"When things come to shut me down or get me to unduly conform, I respond from a place of knowing my purpose."

- James Vincent

NOTES:

_____

_____

_____

_____

_____

_____

_____

_____

_____

_____

_____

_____

_____

_____

_____

_____

_____

_____

_____

_____

_____

_____

_____

Game Break!

As you find the words in this word search, examine your life. Let these words speak to you for personal reflection, inspiration, and advancement.

Power of the Voice

```
S  H  U  T  D  O  W  N  Z  L  E  P  X  F  D  S  U  N  R  R
Q  H  S  W  J  O  K  A  I  E  K  A  G  K  T  N  R  E  F  L
T  O  F  E  A  R  S  M  W  E  E  L  J  U  S  O  S  I  E  A
O  R  L  A  S  D  P  C  M  K  I  R  W  T  B  O  L  I  W  K
V  D  A  V  W  A  E  I  O  M  R  T  O  S  N  T  R  A  Z  R
E  E  W  U  C  T  N  F  I  F  E  P  C  A  E  C  K  Y  M  X
R  T  M  T  M  D  F  T  E  S  P  U  T  R  G  E  U  L  K  Z
C  I  J  E  A  A  L  U  D  A  R  E  S  D  N  G  I  I  P  A
O  B  E  G  I  E  S  N  B  I  T  Z  E  I  S  B  D  K  C  P
M  I  C  M  S  C  I  L  T  U  S  F  N  S  E  E  G  T  I  R
E  H  R  S  Z  M  E  Y  G  L  I  G  U  R  N  D  I  V  M  T
Y  N  E  Y  E  E  V  R  D  N  Q  O  A  T  S  O  G  G  P  N
M  I  I  F  S  J  R  J  I  D  E  T  I  I  N  U  S  J  O  E
H  N  F  I  R  H  Z  N  T  G  E  T  L  S  Y  W  M  D  R  M
O  U  J  L  L  S  G  J  A  D  Y  E  J  T  X  L  K  E  T  E
R  X  Z  P  X  U  G  R  S  F  N  J  U  B  Q  N  A  L  A  V
H  P  R  M  T  G  U  Z  P  C  B  I  Z  J  L  Z  E  A  N  O
T  U  H  A  U  O  Y  N  E  J  O  I  X  Z  L  K  P  E  T  M
O  I  X  V  C  E  M  P  O  W  E  R  M  E  N  T  S  H  U  G
G  O  X  H  L  M  K  L  A  T  E  K  Q  L  G  K  D  Q  Q  C
```

1. Actions	**8.** Defining	**15.** Liberated	**22.** Resonate
2. Awakening	**9.** Empowerment	**16.** Limitless	**23.** Shutdown
3. Amplify	**10.** Fears	**17.** Mind	**24.** Speak
4. Fierce	**11.** Healed	**18.** Mindset	**25.** Silence
5. Filters	**12.** Identity	**19.** Movement	**26.** Traumas
6. Courageous	**13.** Impact	**20.** Obscurity	**27.** Uninhibited
7. Defeat	**14.** Important	**21.** Overcome	**28.** Unstoppable

The Power of the Voice

33

Chapter 6.
Finding Your Voice: The Mask Comes Off

`1. During my teenage years, I was afraid that my own natural voice would be inadequate; therefore I didn't bother to explore it. I think it's safe to say that we don't typically explore those areas where we feel weak. Look over your life and answer these questions. When did you begin to feel that your voice was inadequate? Have you been able to overcome those feelings in regards to that particular instance or area?

_____

_____

_____

_____

_____

_____

POWER POINT

"Any mask we wear is a mask we bear the responsibility for either keeping up or destroying."

- James Vincent

2. Many times we don't seem to want to choose that "genuine" part of us, because we are afraid of what we'll find or what others will think. Give a description below of what the clearest, purest, loudest part of you would look, sound and feel like.

_____

_____

_____

_____

_____

_____

_____

3. Do something RIGHT NOW that you've never done before that represents your letting go and leaving the confines of whatever is restricting or limiting you. Then write it here, along with today's date. This marks the day that you decided to give up the mask completely.

_____

_____

_____

_____

_____

_____

_____

_____

_____

NOTES:

_____

_____

_____

_____

_____

_____

_____

_____

_____

_____

_____

_____

_____

_____

_____

_____

_____

_____

_____

_____

The Power of the Voice

Chapter 7.
Finding Your Voice: The Big Squeeze

1. Sometimes the reason we have a hard time knowing and / or expressing the truth of who we are is the fact that we are not willing to fully immerse ourselves in the process it takes to reach maturity. Have you found yourself looking back at your life and seeing that if you would have stayed in a particular process, you would have added value to your potential? If so, discuss it below.

_____

_____

_____

_____

_____

_____

_____

2. Describe the parallels between cultivating wine grapes and the human experience. What makes them so similar?

_____

_____

_____

_____

_____

_____

_____

3. Why is the "struggle" necessary for the reproduction of wine grapes? What happens to them without a difficult environment? Apply this concept to your own life   as   you   assess.

_____

_____

_____

_____

_____

_____

4. Like the production of grapes, what are the benefits we receive when difficult situations occur in our lives?

_____

_____

_____

_____

_____

_____

POWER POINT

"As I look back on my life, I truly say that, one way or another, every stormy situation I've experienced has created some form of maturity in me and added something to my overall personality and relation to life in general."

- James Vincent

5. As we journey through life, we begin to have deep regrets over certain situations we've experienced and walked through. These circumstances also teach us many lessons. Take a moment to reflect, and ask yourself to look at what you gained from those things you wish never would have happened. *These are the things that cause us to be fruitful in life. Then, be willing to discuss this with others. (This is a great discussion for small groups or clubs.)

_____

_____

_____

_____

_____

_____

_____

_____

<u>POWER POINT</u>

"When we don't take time to healthily reflect on these things, but allow it to fester into something horrible, we develop a huge wall, a silence if you will, that stops us from moving into the next phase of who we are."

- James Vincent

6. Many times when we are feeling *squeezed*, we begin to remove ourselves from the process of maturation and this stunts our growth and productivity. Isolation brings us into a comfortable environment that does not allow for us to be the

The Power of the Voice

greatest expression of who we are. Name some uncomfortable things that we all

should be willing to embrace the greatest expression of ourselves? Once again,

be   willing   to   discuss   with   others.

_____

_____

_____

_____

_____

_____

_____

POWER POINT

"Mature vines naturally make the most complex wine. Likewise, voices that

have been allowed to mature through its natural, unique process convey the

most honest message and sound."

- James Vincent

Answer the questions below for personal reflection and development.

1. What challenges have you faced that have given you a voice for this moment of your life?

_____

_____

_____

2. Is what you've learned helping you at this point on your path?

_____

_____

_____

3. What parts of your journey are difficult to revisit?

_____

_____

_____

_____

_____

4. Are you willing to confront your past and let it benefit you, or let it keep control of a portion of your voice, and weaken your identity?

_____

_____

_____

_____

_____

5. How are you presently being stretched or squeezed ? Or are you somehow avoiding a new maturing process in your life?

_____

_____

_____

_____

_____

_____

_____

GROUP DISCUSSION TOPICS:

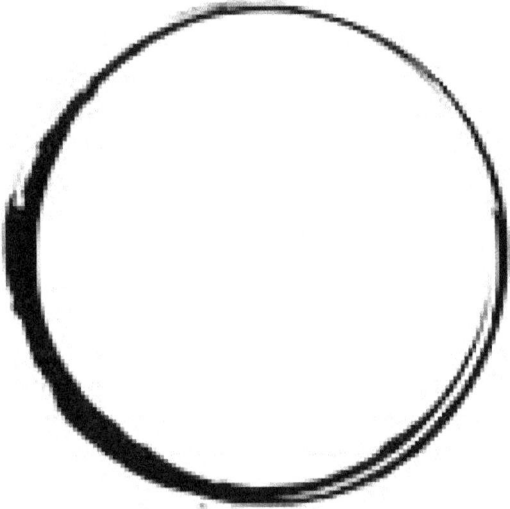

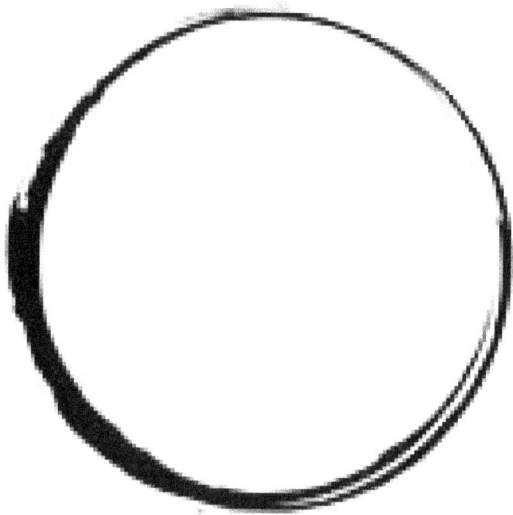

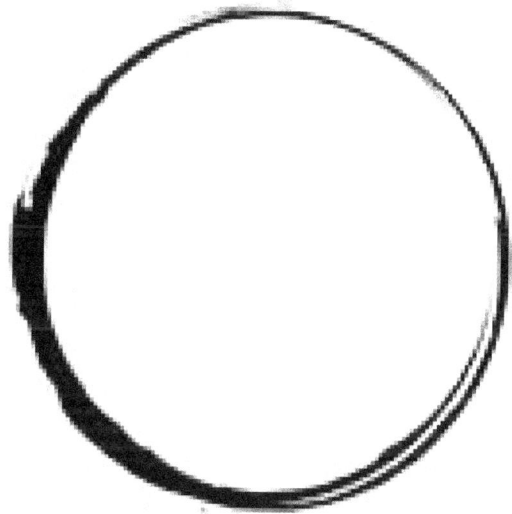

NOTES:

_____

_____

_____

_____

_____

_____

_____

_____

_____

_____

_____

_____

_____

_____

_____

_____

_____

The Power of the Voice

_____

_____

_____

_____

_____

_____

_____

The Power of the Voice

Chapter 8.
Regaining Your Voice: Break Free

1. Your voice is essentially an extension of yourself. When we discover that we actually have something unique to contribute, the realm of possibility expands for us. List some of the things that you can contribute within your sphere of influence by using your voice.

_____

_____

_____

_____

_____

_____

POWER POINT

"The less we want to open our eyes to what's really happening within ourselves, and I mean deep within ourselves, the more likely we are to remain in a space we were not meant to occupy."

- James Vincent

2. As you assess your present position, what areas of your life are you going to lay down all excuses and take full responsibility for to experience a new freedom and clarity?_____

_____

_____

_____

POWER POINT

"I believe our voice needs to have a solid, unshakeable reason to come alive and stay alive...Whatever it is, it's got to go far beyond ourselves and some fleeting desire to make a noise that gives us a meaningless spotlight."

- James Vincent

2. What is a specific thing that causes your voice to come alive? Be willing to share the response to this question with others. This causes you to gain confidence in expressing who you are.

_____

_____

_____

_____

The Power of the Voice

3. *Effective listening* is a very useful tool that empowers the listener to speak confidently. When was the last time you listened to someone, with the genuine intent to take in and process what that person was expressing? Explain.

_____

_____

_____

_____

<u>POWER POINT</u>

"A changing thought pattern is vital to fashioning a lifestyle of liberty. Keep doing the useful things that your mind keeps telling you not to do, and it will eventually change..Sometimes, it's not so much figuring out why your voice is shut down as it is getting out and doing something."

- James Vincent

4. When *voice raiders* show up and are ready to drag you backwards, trying to make you believe that your voice is not worth hearing, what should you do?

_____

_____

_____

_____

_____

_____

POWER POINT

"Understand that your voice, as it is today, is perfect– because it's yours. you're not trying to get a voice– you already have one. it will get stronger and stronger, clearer and clearer, but it's already perfect."

- James Vincent

Do the following to actively use your voice and stay free.

1. Make a list of all the negative things you've said about yourself.

_____

_____

_____

_____

_____

2. Write, then speak out loud whatever is the opposite of those things.

_____

_____

_____

_____

_____

3. Recognize the triggers that cause you to shrink back into a repressed state, and be intentional about using your pure expression as an offensive measure.

4. List every excuse you've ever given yourself to remain timid and ashamed of your true voice, then burn that list, or throw it away. Don't sabotage yourself any longer.

_____

_____

_____

_____

NOTES:

_____

_____

_____

_____

_____

_____

_____

_____

_____

_____

_____

_____

_____

_____

_____

_____

_____

_____

_____

_____

_____

_____

_____

_____

Chapter 9.
The Power of the Voice

1. When we begin moving in the direction of our true expression, we must understand that doesn't mean things will now be glorious from that point onward. We must decide to be the voice-activated version of who we are now. No matter what happens. Now, describe the new empowered version of yourself.

_____ _____

_____

_____

_____

_____

_____

_____

POWER POINT

"Although we don't always see it, everything on our path can be useful to our overall growth. If we'll open our eyes, we discover that most of our experiences add to the power of the voice."

- James Vincent

2. Have you signed an "unwritten contract " with anything that keeps you in a restricted or limited place? Begin assessing your future goals and expectations. List the things you find that you must break agreement with...and set yourself free!

_____ _____

_____

_____

_____

POWER POINT

"You have the power to break agreement with everything that wants to imprison you. If the "opposing force" is trying to force you to go left, then take the risk and go right."

- James Vincent

3. Receiving and giving love is a vital substance of human life. Love nourishes, liberates and empowers the very fabric of our being. What are some actionable steps that you will take to let love be expressed in your life in new ways?

_____

_____

POWER POINT

"Love is so much more than an emotion or feeling; it involves the limits someone will go to in order to see you be the best you that you can be...Love is power."

- James Vincent

NOTES:

_____

_____

_____

_____

_____

_____

_____

_____

_____

_____

_____

_____

_____

_____

_____

_____

_____

_____

The Power of the Voice

THE STORY OF A NEW BEGINNING

Write the new narrative for the newly-empowered you.

_____

_____

_____

_____

_____

_____

_____

_____

_____

_____

_____

_____

_____

_____

_____

_____

_____

_____

_____

_____

_____

_____

_____

_____

_____

_____

_____

_____

_____

The Power of the Voice

Fill in the circles by describing the areas of your life that will become brighter when you begin to use your voice.

Then target those areas.

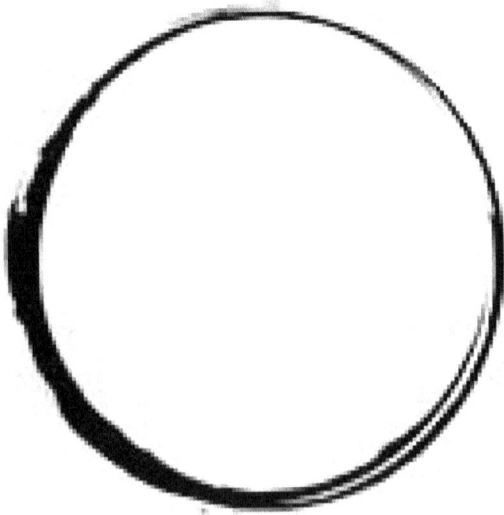

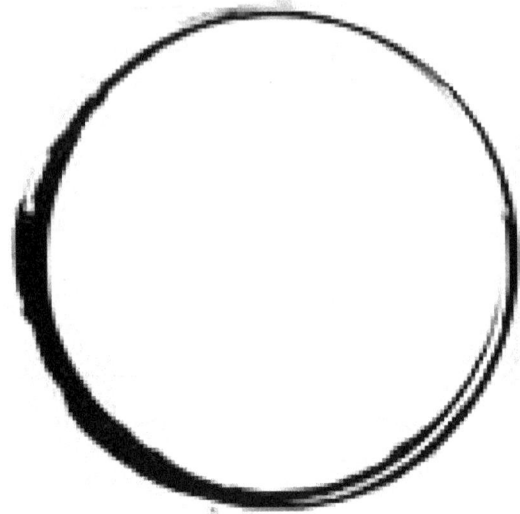

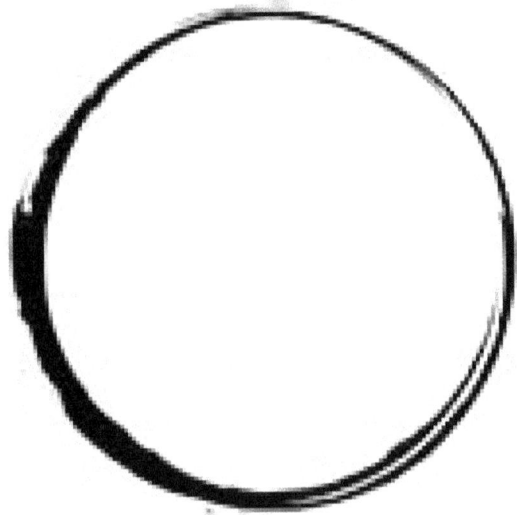

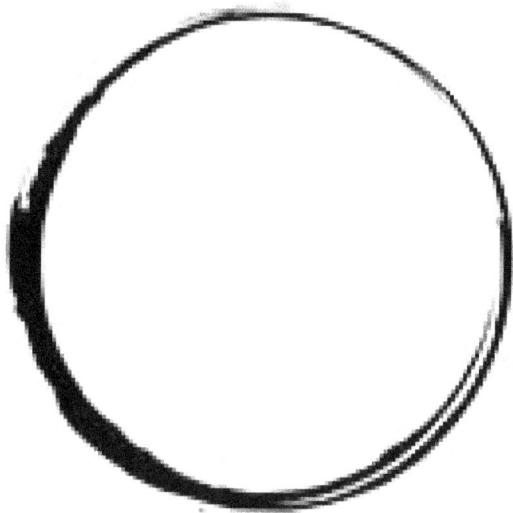

GOALS AND ASPIRATIONS:

_____

_____

_____

_____

_____

_____

_____

_____

_____

_____

_____

_____

_____

_____

_____

_____

The Power of the Voice

_____

_____

_____

_____

_____

The Power of the Voice

AFFIRMATIONS:

1. I AM AN AMAZING, BRILLIANT, AND UNIQUE INDIVIDUAL.

2. MY VOICE IS IMPORTANT. I AM THE ONLY ONE IN THE WORLD WHO SOUNDS LIKE ME.

3. MY PRESENCE CAN NEVER BE UNDERESTIMATED.

4. MY VOICE AND TALENTS ARE POWER TOOLS FOR ANY SITUATION.

5. NOTHING CAN STOP, HINDER, OR PREVENT ME FROM BEING WHO I AM.

6. I AM HERE IN THIS WORLD FOR A REASON, AND MY MISTAKES, FAILURES, OR SHORTCOMINGS HAVE NOTHING TO DO WITH IT.

7. WHEN I OPEN MY MOUTH THINGS CHANGE.

8. MY SOUND IS BEAUTIFUL! IT IS DISTINCT AND FREE.

9. MY VOICE CAN BUILD SUCCESS, CREATE OPPORTUNITIES & GIVE SOLUTIONS.

NOW, TAKE TIME TO WRITE YOUR OWN AFFIRMATIONS.

_____

_____

_____

_____

_____

The Power of the Voice

The Power of the Voice

The Power of the Voice

THE CONCLUSION...

"The sound in you is being awakened to cause movement within you and around you. This stirring in you is strengthening your faith in yourself and what you believe. You are discovering the inherent purpose that has been ready to manifest. The path is yours; the story is yours. The voice is awake and it's getting ready to roar...are you ready?"

Let's go!

- *The Power of the Voice*

www.ingramcontent.com/pod-product-compliance
Lightning Source LLC
Chambersburg PA
CBHW081259040426
42452CB00014B/2577